Cats Rule!

Favourite CAT BREEDS

Persians, Abyssinians, Siamese, Sphynx and all the Breeds In-Between

by Angie Peterson Kaelberer

raintree

a Capstone company — publishers for children

Raintree is an imprint of Capstone Global Library Limited, a company incorporated in England and Wales having its registered office at 264 Banbury Road, Oxford, OX2 7DY– Registered company number: 6695582

www.raintree.co.uk
myorders@raintree.co.uk

Text © Capstone Global Library Limited 2017
The moral rights of the proprietor have been asserted.

Edited by Carrie Sheely,
Designed by Philippa Jer~
Illustrated by HL Studio~
Original illustrations © (
Picture research by Svet~
Production by Steve Wal~
Originated by Capstone
Printed and bound in Ch~~~~

...Services p. 26

ISBN 978 1 4747 1291 0 (hardback)
19 18 17 16 15
10 9 8 7 6 5 4 3 2 1

ISBN 978 1 4747 1723 6 (paperback)
20 19 18 17 16
10 9 8 7 6 5 4 3 2 1

British Library Cataloguing in Publication Data
A full catalogue record for this book is available from the British Library.

Acknowledgements
We would like to thank the following for permission to reproduce photographs: Capstone Press: Philippa Jenkins, back cover and throughout; Dreamstime: Brittneygobble, 27, Linda Johnsonbaugh, 25; Getty Images: SSPL, 5; Newscom: AdMedia/Birdie Thompson, 12, Europics, 14 (top), facebook/blindcathoneybee/ZJAN, 17 (top), Zuma Press/Caters News, 20; Shutterstock: bonzodog, 15, Chris Rinckes, 19, cynoclub, 23, Daria Filimonova, 13, Dmitry Maslov, 21, Eric Isselee, cover (front and middle), 14 (bottom), Ewais, 8, 18 (bottom), Jaguar PS, 18 (top), Kirill Vorobyev, cover (left), klom, 10, Krissi Lundgren, 22, Lisa A, 29, nelik, 11, Rob Hainer, 17 (bottom), Sarah Fields Photography, 4, Vladyslav Starozhylov, 6

The author would like to thank Laurie Patton, Regional Director, TICA Southeast, for her invaluable help in the preparation of this book.

Disclaimer
All the internet addresses (URLs) given in this book were valid at the time of going to press. However, due to the dynamic nature of the internet, some addresses may have changed, or sites may have changed or ceased to exist since publication. While the author and publishers regret any inconvenience this may cause readers, no responsibility for any such changes can be accepted by either the author or the publishers.

Some words are shown in bold, **like this**. You can find out what they mean by looking in the glossary.

Contents

CHAPTER 1

It's a cat's world

According to an old saying, dogs are man's best friend. But we certainly love cats, too! At least 7.9 million pet cats live in the United Kingdom, compared to about 9 million dogs. Many pet owners prefer cats because they don't require as much space as many dog breeds. Cats also don't need to be taken outside for walks.

Cats and their owners share a special bond. If you have had a rotten day, your cat is there to purr, rub against your legs, cuddle on your lap or just listen.

Cats were an important part of ancient Egyptian culture. Ancient Egyptians mummified cats as well as human bodies.

Cat history

Scientists believe the domestic cat probably developed around 9,000 years ago from an African wildcat called *felis silvestris lybica*. At that time, people kept cats mainly because they killed mice, rats and other rodents. Cats later moved into people's homes as pets. Mummified cats have been found in the tombs of wealthy and important ancient Egyptians dating back to 1500 BC. Ancient Egyptians admired cats. The Egyptian goddess Bastet had a cat's head and a woman's body.

As ancient people moved into new areas, they took their cats with them. By the AD 1400s cats reached the New World on the ships of European explorers. In North and South America, they continued to keep their owners' homes free from pests.

🐾 Cat breeds galore!

Cats don't have as many differences in size and physical features as dogs. That's one reason why people don't always realize that there are many cat breeds. Like dogs, cat breeds are different in both appearance and personality. Cat breeds can have short hair, long hair – or almost no hair! Some breeds love to play with their owners and be involved in whatever they're doing, while others are more independent.

The earliest cat breeds are considered natural breeds because they came about with little or no influence from humans. These breeds, which include the Persian, Siamese, Turkish Angora, Egyptian Mau and Burmese, date back as far as 3,000 years ago. By the late 1800s, cats were popular pets throughout Europe. Owners began breeding cats to produce kittens with certain **traits** or even to produce entirely new breeds. A cat show at London's Crystal Palace in 1871 increased the popularity of several breeds, including the Siamese, Abyssinian and British Shorthair.

Today, nearly 100 cat breeds exist. About half of them are recognized by cat breed associations. These breeds can compete for breed championship awards in cat shows. Cat breed associations include the Cat Fanciers' Association (CFA) and The International Cat Association (TICA).

Most popular breeds, Cat Fanciers' Association	
1	Exotic
2	Persian
3	Maine Coon
4	Ragdoll
5	British Shorthair
6	American Shorthair
7	Abyssinian
8	Sphynx
9	Siamese
10	Scottish Fold

Most popular breeds, The International Cat Association	
1	Bengal
2	Ragdoll
3	Maine Coon
4	Persian
5	Sphynx
6	Siamese
7	Himalayan
8	Siberian
9	Norwegian Forest
10	Abyssinian

trait quality or characteristic that makes one person or animal different from another

CHAPTER 2

Short-haired breeds

Putting up with cat hair on your clothes and furniture is part of owning a cat. But short cat hairs are usually easier to clean up than long cat hairs. Short-haired breeds also don't need daily brushing and combing. If you're looking for a more low-maintenance cat, a shorthair is probably a good choice.

🐾 British Shorthair

Have you ever heard of a cat invasion? The British Shorthair may be descended from cats that travelled to Britain with Roman invaders about 2,000 years ago.

The British Shorthair is a sturdy cat with a large, round head and wide eyes. Their coats can be almost any colour or pattern, from solid to tricoloured to tabby. British Shorthairs are known for their calm, quiet personalities. They are affectionate but don't demand attention from their owners.

Because they are calm and quiet, British Shorthair cats are great family pets.

Colourful cats

Cats have many colours and patterns. Even a single litter of kittens can contain cats with several different colours. The three most common colour patterns are solid, tabby and pointed, although different breeds may have different colour standards.

Cat colouring and patterns		
solid	one colour throughout	
bicolour	white and one colour	
colourpoint	light-coloured bodies with a darker colour or pattern on the face, ears, legs and tail	
tabby	lighter main colour with darker stripes or spots	
calico	patches of two or more colours, such as black, tan or orange	
tortoiseshell	black with patches of orange	
ticked	each hair has alternating light and dark bands	
van	white coat with a coloured tail and splashes of colour between the ears	

🐾 American Shorthair

This breed began with British Shorthair cats that travelled from Europe with some of the first colonists to the New World in the early 1600s. Breeders chose beautiful cats with good personalities and certain colours to create a new breed. In 1966 this new breed was named the American Shorthair.

American Shorthairs are similar in looks and personality to their British cousins. Their coats come in nearly every colour or pattern, with the silver, or grey, tabby being one of the most common.

Did you know?

What if all blondes were girls and all redheads were boys? Something like that happens in the cat world. Nearly all calico and tortoiseshell cats are female, and most red or orange tabbies are male.

American Shorthair cats are gentle companions.

Abyssinians love to play and have a lot of energy.

🐾 Abyssinian

Those who prefer dogs to cats will probably get along well with the Abyssinian. These cats are social and like being involved in whatever their owners are doing. Instead of being shy with strangers, they'll run to the door to greet visitors. Many even enjoy playing games of fetch! They love to climb and their energy level remains high after they grow into adulthood. If you want a cat that snoozes in the sunshine all day, an Abyssinian probably isn't for you.

People often say that Abyssinians look like little pumas. Their coats are ticked. Each hair has bands of light and dark hair, similar to wildcat coats. Their bodies are long and slender. Coat colours include ruddy (brown), red (orange), blue (grey) and fawn (beige).

Abyssinians got their name from the country of Abyssinia, which today is called Ethiopia. But no one is sure if the cats' ancestors actually came from Ethiopia. Most cat experts believe the breed began in the late 1800s in Britain. In 1871 Abyssinians were part of the first cat show at the Crystal Palace in London.

LIL BUB

Lil Bub is a tiny brown tabby adopted from an animal shelter. She has a kitten-like appearance, even though she's an adult. Lil Bub was the smallest in her litter and had to be bottle-fed. Her tongue sticks out because she has a short lower jaw. She also has a bone disorder that caused her growth to be stunted.

Siamese

Would you like to have a conversation with your cat? If so, the Siamese is the breed for you! They are one of the most vocal breeds. If you speak to a Siamese, it's likely to reply with a loud "miaow".

The Siamese is one of the oldest cat breeds. It began in Thailand, which was once called Siam. In the early 1870s, the rest of the world got to know Siamese cats when they were part of a cat show in London.

Siamese are famous for their light-coloured coats with darker fur on the tail, paws and ears. These darker areas are called points. Point colours include seal (dark brown), chocolate (medium brown), blue (dark grey) and lilac (pale grey).

The Siamese is one of the most social breeds. They don't like to spend a lot of time alone. If you're unable to be at home most of the day, you should get another pet as a friend for your Siamese.

Seal Point Siamese cats have very dark points on their faces, ears, tails and paws.

Did you know?

All Siamese kittens are born with white coats. The points appear after a few weeks and reach full colour after a few months. Siamese carry a **gene** that is sensitive to heat. The body parts where the point colours appear are cooler than the rest of the body. A Siamese in a cooler climate will have darker points than one in a warmer climate.

gene part of every cell that carries physical and behavioural information passed from parents to their offspring

SNOOPY

Snoopy is an Exotic from China. His plush coat and wide eyes make him look like a stuffed toy. His owner posts many photos of him on the internet, usually wearing bandannas, ties and other accessories.

🐾 Exotic

The Exotic is an American breed. It began in the 1960s when breeders crossed long-haired Persians with American Shorthairs, Burmese and Russian Blues. These breeders wanted a cat with the Persian's appearance and personality, but a shorter coat. The Exotic's face is similar to a Persian, but it has a plush, short coat that's easier to groom.

An Exotic has a sturdy body, short legs and a round head. Its large, round eyes give it a sweet look. Its soft coat can be any colour or pattern.

If you want a cuddly cat, an Exotic is a great choice. Its nickname is the "teddy bear cat". Exotics love to curl up in their owner's lap for a nap or to be stroked.

Did you know?

In 2014 the Exotic became the CFA's number one cat breed. It took over the top spot from the Persian, which had been there since the 1970s.

Exotic cats love the company of others, including other pets.

14

Sphynx

Perhaps you don't want to deal with cat hair at all. In that case, the Sphynx could be your perfect pet.

Sphynx are known as hairless cats, but their bodies are usually covered with a light **down** that's difficult to see. Their skin feels soft and can be a number of different colours and patterns. They have rounded bodies and large ears.

The breed began as a genetic **mutation** with several hairless kittens born in the 1960s and 1970s. Those cats and their offspring were crossed with Devon Rex cats, which have very short hair, to create the Sphynx.

Because of their lack of thick fur, Sphynx get cold and sunburned easily. And even though they don't shed any hairs, their bodies still need care. Their skin produces oil, so they need to be bathed occasionally and wiped daily with a soft, damp cloth.

down soft, light hair on a human or animal
mutataion natural, unexpected change in a gene

CHAPTER 3

Long-haired breeds

Many people find long-haired cats especially attractive. However, most long-haired breeds need to be combed or brushed daily to keep their long hair from forming **mats**.

🐾 Himalayan

What do you get when you cross a Persian with a Siamese? A Himalayan! This cat has the long, silky coat of a Persian with the blue eyes and point markings of a Siamese.

Himalayans have been described as combining the best features of both breeds. They are more active than Persians, but quieter and calmer than the typical Siamese.

Did you know?

The Birman cat looks a lot like the Himalayan. However, it has four white paws and its body is longer and less compact than that of the Himalayan or Persian. The Birman's coat also isn't as thick, so it's easier to groom.

mat thick, tangled mass of hair

HONEY BEE

Honey Bee is a blind calico cat. As a kitten, Honey Bee had a painful eye condition that resulted in the loss of both eyes. Although Honey Bee can't see, she goes on hikes with her family. She walks on a lead and travels around in her owner's rucksack.

Himalayans are affectionate pets.

GRUMPY CAT

TV and social media star Grumpy Cat's real name is Tardar Sauce. Her owner says she's not really grumpy – her expression comes from the fact that she's a **dwarf** cat. Her markings are similar to a Himalayan or Ragdoll, but her parents were a calico and a grey tabby.

 Persian

The Persian's sweet expression, soft coat and gentle personality have made it a popular breed since the late 1800s. Until 2014 it was the CFA's most popular breed for more than 30 years.

Like Exotics, Persians have sturdy bodies, short legs, round heads and large eyes. However, their coats are long and flowing. Long fur around the Persian's neck forms a **ruff** that looks a bit like a lion's mane. The ruff, along with the underbelly and tail, need extra grooming to keep them free of mats.

Persians are among the quietest cats. When they do miaow, it's soft and low. They're affectionate and love to cuddle.

Persians have sweet and gentle personalities.

Ragdolls are laid-back and well-behaved pets.

 Ragdoll

The Ragdoll breed came to the UK in the 1980s. Its name comes from its tendency to completely relax when picked up – becoming as soft and limp as a rag doll. The Ragdoll enjoys being around people. Its gentle, affectionate personality makes it a good pct for families with children.

Ragdolls are one of the largest cat breeds and can weigh more than 9 kilograms (20 pounds). They grow more slowly than most cat breeds, reaching thcir full size at about the age of four.

Many Ragdolls have point markings. Somc arc mitted, which means that they have white front paws and white back legs up to the knee. Others have bicolour patterns. While their hair is long, it doesn't tangle easily. Two or three brushings each week is enough.

dwarf animal or plant that is smaller than the usual size for its type or species
ruff ring of long hair around an animal's neck

19

🐾 Maine Coon

This breed developed naturally in the eastern United States in the 1800s. No one is sure of the breed's history, but long-haired cats that travelled on ships from Europe may have mated with short-haired cats already living in the area.

The Maine Coon is the official state cat breed of Maine, USA. These large cats get their name from the state and also from their long, fluffy tails, which look a lot like those of raccoons.

Maine Coons are long and muscular. They can weigh as much as 9 kilograms (20 pounds). But the miaow of this gentle giant sounds more like a chirp. They are social and playful.

Maine Coons can be almost any colour or pattern, with tabby being the most common. Their coats have two layers. The outer layer helps repel water and the inner layer keeps the cat's body warm. The fur doesn't mat easily and needs to be combed only occasionally.

MARU

Maru is a Scottish Fold from Japan. He's the star of many internet videos. He often tries to squeeze or jump into a small box.

A fluffy Maine Coon's coat is silky but oily.

CHAPTER 4

New and unique

Serengeti

Are you ready to walk on the wild side? Most new breeds are created from two or more established breeds. But some breeders go back to the domestic cat's wild cousins to develop new breeds. These **hybrid** breeds are a much-debated issue in the cat world. Many people say that wildcat traits and behaviour don't belong in a domestic pet. Others like the hybrids' unique appearance and high energy.

Serengeti

If you like the look of a wildcat, then the Serengeti may be for you. This cat has a spotted coat, long legs and large ears like a wildcat. But it is smaller and has a calmer personality.

The Serengeti breed began in the 1990s when breeders crossed Oriental cats with Bengals. They created a sociable cat that likes to climb. Like Siamese, the Serengeti is vocal and likes to have "conversations" with its owner.

hybrid plant or animal that has been bred from two different species or varieties

The most popular Bengal colour is a brown and black tabby.

🐾 Bengal

The Bengal breed began in the 1960s when scientist Jean S. Mill crossed a domestic cat with a small wildcat called an Asian leopard cat. The wildcat is immune to **feline leukaemia**. Mill and her colleague Dr Willard Centerwall hoped to produce a cat that would also be immune to the disease. That didn't happen, but other breeders continued this work. They crossed the Asian Leopard Cat with popular domestic cats such as British and American Shorthairs, Bombays and Egyptian Maus. By the 1980s the Bengal was an established breed.

Bengals are large and muscular, weighing up to 7 kilograms (15 pounds). Their coats are a mixture of spotted and tabby markings. These energetic cats need lots of playtime with their owners. Otherwise, curtains and treasured belongings can turn into Bengal toys. Even a Bengal with wildcats as distant descendants will display some wild behaviours.

feline leukaemia disease in cats caused by a virus; feline leukaemia causes weight loss, infections and eventually death

Savannah

Probably the hybrid closest to its wild roots, the Savannah is one of the newest cat breeds. It began in 1986 when a breeder crossed a domestic female Siamese with a male **serval**. The cat had one kitten, which the breeder named Savannah, after the African grasslands where the serval lives.

The Savannah gets its spotted coat, large ears and hooded eyes from its serval ancestors. It loves to climb, and its long legs help it leap up to 2.5 metres (8 feet). Unlike many breeds, the Savannah often enjoys playing in water.

Like Bengals, Savannahs are social cats and need lots of playtime. Savannah owners should "cat-proof" their homes by putting away breakable objects and covering power cables. Savannahs are intelligent, and many work out how to turn on taps or open cupboards and drawers.

generation all the members of a group of people or animals born around the same time
serval long-legged African wildcat with a spotted coat

Savannahs are known for their ability to jump.

Lykoi

Do you like scary stories? Then you just might like the look of one of the newest cat breeds, the Lykoi. Its rough coat and hairless patches make it look like a werewolf!

The Lykoi isn't a hybrid. It's a domestic cat with a recessive gene. Some **feral** cats produced kittens that were born solid black but soon lost hair on areas of their bodies. The remaining fur turned to a mixture of black and white hairs. Other kittens were born without any hair at all. Breeders had the kittens tested to make sure the hairlessness wasn't caused by a disease. Then they began breeding them with black cats to produce the Lykoi.

The Lykoi has little to no hair on the back of its ears or around the eyes, chin or nose. Most have little hair on their legs and paws. They have intelligent personalities and enjoy "hunting" for toys and playing games of fetch. Lykois don't warm up quickly to new people or animals. But once you win their trust, they are very loyal.

feral wild, or in a wild state

A Lykoi may shed its hair and then regrow it later in its ife.

Which cat breed is best for you?

Choosing a cat

Small or large? Short-haired or long-haired? Friendly or independent? All of these characteristics and more are found in our feline friends. Doing some research on what you and your family want in a cat will help you find the breed that's the purr-fect match!

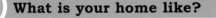

1 What is your home like?

a. My mum has a million fragile ornaments.
b. Our house is uncluttered and simple.
c. My family can't stand dust anywhere!

2 How do you want to spend time with your pet?

a. I could cuddle with my cat all day every day.
b. I want to play fetch and other games with my cat every day.
c. I will love my pets, but I am involved in lots of activities.

3 How do you feel about grooming your cat?

a. I would like brushing my cat every day – it's a great way to bond.
b. My hair is low maintenance – I want the same for my cat.
c. I don't want to brush my cat – ever.

4 Is anyone in your family allergic to animal hair?

a. No, not at all.
b. A little sneezing once in a while, but nothing too serious.
c. Yes – very allergic!

Mostly As: Your perfect cat is a Persian, Ragdoll or Himalayan.
Mostly Bs: Your perfect cat is a Siamese, Abyssinian or Bengal.
Mostly Cs: Your perfect cat is a Sphynx.

Answers

Cat grass garden

Many cats love to eat grass, and will happily snack on the lawn in your garden. If you live in a flat, or don't have a garden or outside space – don't worry! You can grow you own cat grass inside.

What you need:

- medium-size flowerpot with a drainage saucer
- potting compost or organic soil
- 1 packet of cat grass seeds, available from pet shops or garden centres
- small watering can filled with water

What to do:

1. Fill the flowerpot about ¾ full with soil.

2. Use your fingers to poke five to seven holes in the soil.

3. Sprinkle about five seeds in each hole.

4. Cover the holes with about ½ centimetre (¼ inch) of soil.

5. Water the pot lightly, and place it on a sunny window sill. Keep the soil moist. The seeds should sprout within one to two weeks. When the grass grows to about 6 centimetres, it's ready for your cat to eat!

Glossary

down soft, light hair on a human or animal

dwarf animal or plant that is smaller than the usual size for its type or species

feline leukaemia disease in cats caused by a virus; feline leukaemia causes weight loss, infections and eventually death

feral wild, or in a wild state

gene part of every cell that carries physical and behavioural information passed from parents to their offspring

generation all the members of a group of people or animals born around the same time

hybrid plant or animal that has been bred from two different species or varieties

mat thick, tangled mass of hair

mutation natural, unexpected change in a gene

ruff ring of long hair around an animal's neck

serval long-legged African wildcat with a spotted coat

trait quality or characteristic that makes one person or animal different from another

Books

Animal Classification: Do Cats Have Family Trees?
(Show Me Science), Eve Hartman and Wendy Meshbesher
(Raintree, 2014)

Caring for Cats and Kittens (Battersea Dogs & Cats Home
Pet Care Guides), Ben Hubbard (Franklin Watts, 2015)

Cats (Animal Family Albums), Charlotte Guillain
(Raintree, 2013)

The Complete Cat Breed Book, DK
(Dorling Kindersley, 2013)

 **Websites**

www.cats.org.uk/cat-care/cats-for-kids
Find out some fascinating feline facts, take part in fun
activities and games and get useful cat care advice.

www.rspca.org.uk/adviceandwelfare/pets/cats
Find out more about cat behaviour and welfare.

🐾 Comprehension questions

1. How are domestic cats and wildcats similar? Which breeds share the most in common with wildcats?

2. Why did humans tame cats? Did the relationship between cats and humans benefit one or the other more, or did both benefit equally?

3. Some cat breed characteristics and traits are developed naturally. Others come from humans breeding cats. Which do you think is better for the cat? Why?

Index